Contents

5 *Welcome*

7 SECTION 1: *Great news*
Aims to help you grasp what God has done for us through Jesus. It unpacks the Bible's main message (as set out in the book of Romans) and makes clear what becoming a Christian is all about.

15 SECTION 2: *Face the music*
Confronts you with what Jesus himself said to those who wanted to follow him. It's uncomfortable reading, but vital to take in early on. All the readings are taken from Luke's gospel.

21 SECTION 3: *Get up and grow*
Explains practically, using the book of Colossians, how to make progress as one of God's people, trusting Jesus. What's the way forward day by day?

29 SECTION 4: *Great expectations*
What's it like following Christ? Satisfying, difficult, enjoyable—or all three? Discover from the book of 1 Peter what to expect in the Christian life.

35 SECTION 5: *Help!*
Covers questions commonly asked by those who've just become Christians or those investigating Jesus and the Bible. Such as: 'What if I sin really badly?' or 'Can we trust the Bible?' Answers to these and other questions could just stop you from getting tripped up along the way.

Welcome

The big idea

The aim of **Start** is to help you sort out what it is to *become* a Christian and then what it is to *be* one.

It's written for people who want to find out about Jesus and for those who have just become Christians. It will also help anyone who's confused or intrigued about these matters. Whichever your situation, we want to help you get things clear and get started as a Christian.

The Bible says that it is vital you take this seriously. These matters are critically and eternally significant, as we'll see in the next few pages. Choosing to become a Christian is by far the most important and exciting step you'll ever take.

Al Horn

The small print

You can use ***Start*** on your own, with a friend or in a group. You'll find things are easier if you remember the following:

- Each study page in ***Start*** looks at part of the Bible and asks some questions about it. We use mainly the parts of the Bible called Romans, Luke, Colossians and 1 Peter. Check the 'table of contents' in your Bible to find out where they are.
- Each Bible book is divided up into chapters and verses. So when you see a reference like "Colossians 2 v6-7", then you'll need to find verses 6-7 of the second chapter of Colossians.
- Sometimes we write: "v6a". That means the first half of verse 6; likewise, if we write "v6b" we mean the second half of verse 6.
- In ***Start***, we use and quote from the New International Version of the Bible. It would make sense for you to use this version too.
- Some pages have a longer Bible passage to read, some have more questions. Tackle them at your own pace and in a way you can take in thoughtfully. One a day could be about right if you are using ***Start*** by yourself.
- Feel free to write answers, questions, thoughts and anything else in this book as you go along.
- The Bible is more than just a good read. It's the way that God speaks to us today. And therefore it's a good idea to ask God to teach you and help you understand what you read. Talking to God may be something new to you—you may not even be sure that there is a God out there who's listening! But God loves to answer our prayers—even if it's a hesitant start like this: "Um, I'm not sure that there's Anyone out there, but if there is, please show yourself to me as I read this bit of the Bible."
- When you've completed each page, take the time to absorb the Bible truths, to thank God for what you've learnt, and to ask him to help you change as a result.
- When you've finished ***Start***, we've listed some ideas at the end for what you might do next.

Now, let's get started…

Great news

We'll begin with the momentous news that is the Bible's central message. It's often called the 'gospel' (which is an old fashioned word for 'momentous news'), and it is all about what God has done through Jesus Christ.

We'll learn truths about God, Jesus and ourselves—and see the far-reaching consequences of what God has done.

All the readings in this section come from the New Testament letter to the Romans. It was written by a converted Jew named Paul, who was chosen by Jesus to be a unique messenger for him.

.... SECTION 1

ABOUT... GOD
Romans 1 v18-20

THINK

- What reasons do people give for saying there is a God?

- What reasons do others give for saying there isn't?

- If there is a God, how do we know what he might be like?

Today's Bible passage helps answer these three questions.

READ
Romans 1 v18-20.

ANSWER
Does the passage cast any light on the three questions above?

- What are the right conclusions to draw from looking at the world around us (v19-20)?

- Where does that leave everybody (v20)?

- Why is that a serious position to be in (v18)?

List all that v18-20 teach us about:

- God's existence:

- God's character:

- God's ability:

- God's relationship to the world:

GRASP
The way the world and human beings are made points clearly to the powerful God who made everything. So it's rather stupid to say we can't know if there's a God. He's made it clear.

And it's just as stupid to ignore him: the rest of the Bible shows that God made us to enjoy a relationship with him, living under his loving rule. This is life at its best.

But it's more than just silly to live in God's world as if he didn't rule. It's dangerous. Verse 18 says that such behaviour makes God angry. More on this in the next study…

SUMMARY
God made the world and rules it.

APPLY
- How do these verses change your thinking?

- What's the right response to God now?

ABOUT... US
Romans 3 v10-18

THINK

- *What do this week's newspaper stories or television shows suggest to us is the world's biggest problem?*

- *Would you agree?*

God rules. He created the world and made us to live in his world, recognising he's in charge. Do people do that?

In Romans chapter 3, Paul argues that every human being (Jew and non-Jew) is in the same grim situation.

READ

Romans 3 v9-20.

'Under sin' (v9b) = burdened and trapped by wrongdoing
'Righteous' (v10) = living fully as God wants; being 'right' before him
'The law' (v19a) = the whole Old Testament

ANSWER

Count how often v10-12 say 'no-one…'

Summarise God's verdict from that.

Use v13-15 and 18 to list all the ways we oppose God:

- *Where does that leave absolutely everybody (v16-17, 19b)?*

- *How would you now answer the questions at the start (under 'Think')?*

GRASP

It's worse than pushing your granny down the stairs. Every human being opposes God, elbows him out of the picture and opts to go solo. We want to run our lives our own way. Every bit of us reflects this defiance: speech, actions, mind, will, emotions, and conscience.

We may show our opposition to God in different ways (some of us openly challenge him, while most just ignore him) but we're all guilty of it. More in the next study on the consequences.

SUMMARY

Every human being chooses to oppose God.

APPLY

- *How easy/hard do you find it to accept this verdict?*

- *Why must we?*

ABOUT...
CONSEQUENCES (i)
Romans 6 v23

THINK

Tick your response below to the following statement:

> 'I'm not perfect, but then who is? The point is I'm not that bad and I can't believe in a God who's got a problem with me.'

○ **Agree**   ○ **Disagree**   ○ **Not sure**

- *What are your reasons?*

When we oppose God's rule (what the Bible calls 'sin'), there are serious consequences. Romans chapter 6 spells them out.

READ
Romans 6 v20-23 twice.

ANSWER
Chapter 6 talks of slaves and masters. Complete the box below:

Two masters: v20:	v22:
Two outcomes: v23a:	v23b:

One master (sin) pays wages (what's deserved), the other (God) presents a gift (what's not deserved).

- *What does it mean that sin earns us death?*

GRASP
Elsewhere in the Bible, we see that death means separation from God. God's punishment for our opposition to him is to separate us from himself, both now and after we die (see, for example, 2 Thessalonians 1 v8-9).

Is this fair? Yes. God gives us what we choose: if we don't want anything to do with God now, that's what we'll get in eternity.

- *What does v23b also suggest is possible?*

- *So what might becoming a Christian be all about?*

There's no man-made way back to God. Our sin earns us only separation from him. But v23b speaks of a gift from God: eternal life. Life with him forever. More on this next.

SUMMARY
God rightly separates us from him, now and forever.

APPLY

- *What does this verse teach us about God?*

- *Why is our sin so serious?*

- *Which master do you serve?*

ABOUT... JESUS (i)
Romans 5 v6-11

THINK

True or False? Jesus Christ's death 2000 years ago was...

a) a deserved execution;
b) an assassination;
c) a miscarriage of justice;
d) God's intention;
e) just another death.

The wages of sin is death, we learnt. But eternal life is on offer from God. Romans chapter 5 tells us how that is possible.

READ

Romans 5 v6-11.

ANSWER

Find, and explain, the four descriptions of us:
  v6a
  v6b
  v8
  v10

Find the four descriptions of what God has done through Jesus Christ:
  v6
  v8
  v9
  v10

Find, and explain, the four consequences of the cross:
  v9a
  v9b
  v10
  v11

- What does the cross tell us about ourselves and God (v8)?

GRASP

We each oppose God's rule and become God's enemy (v10a). That makes God angry ('wrath', v9) and he must separate us from himself. From this we can't save ourselves ('powerless', v6).

But there's a God-given way back to him. Out of love, God provided one man, who never opposed God or deserved death, who willingly took our place: God's Son, Jesus. He took responsibility for our sin and paid the death penalty we deserve. Separated from God. For us.

And Jesus' death isn't the end of the story. That's next.

To be a Christian means that I trust his death (and nothing I do) to bring me into relationship with God. More about this later on.

SUMMARY

God sent Jesus to die, to be separated from God his Father, for us.

APPLY

- Why is Jesus' death essential if we're to be forgiven by God?

- What truths about God do these verses bring home?

ABOUT... JESUS (ii)
Romans 1 v1-5

THINK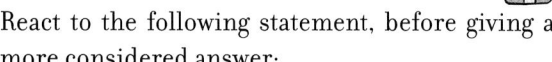

React to the following statement, before giving a more considered answer:

> 'Believing in God makes no sense, let alone trusting in Jesus' death.'

- *What's your first reaction?*

- *What's your more considered opinion?*

Incredibly, Jesus' death wasn't the last word about him, as Paul's introduction to Romans tells us.

READ
Romans 1 v1-5.

ANSWER
Paul introduces himself (v1, 5) as an apostle of Jesus: i.e., one sent by him to declare this 'momentous news' (or gospel) to others.

- *Whose gospel is it, according to Paul (v1b)?*

- *Who is it about (v3a)?*

- *What does the gospel announce about Jesus? (v3-4)?*

GRASP.

In the Old Testament, God promised that a descendant of Israel's great king David would be the 'Messiah', God's chosen rescuer and ruler of the world. The Old Testament also says this figure would be no less than God's Son.

Verse 4 tells us that it is Jesus, and we can know that for sure because God raised him from the dead.

- *What is Jesus' status now (v4b)? What does that mean?*

- *What's the right response to make to him (v5b)?*

The books of Matthew, Mark, Luke, John and Acts tell how Jesus' followers saw him after his resurrection. We can't now see Jesus; he has returned to heaven. But he is alive and unique in the universe. As the one who conquered death, Jesus is Lord. He rules!

SUMMARY

God raised Jesus to declare him Rescuer and Lord of all.

APPLY

- *Why does believing in God and trusting in Jesus make good sense?*

- *How do the historical facts of Jesus' death and resurrection help us in any thinking or discussion about God?*

- *Since Jesus has risen from the dead, how will this affect the way you relate to him now?*

ABOUT...
CONSEQUENCES (ii)
Romans 10 v12-13

THINK

Finish these lines:

> 'Trusting in Jesus is important because…'
> 'Trusting in Jesus is exciting because…'

Jesus died and was raised. Romans 10 shows what follows.

READ

Romans 10 v12-13 twice.

ANSWER

Paraphrase the promise of v13 in your own words.

Then spot the words in v12-13 which show…

a) who this promise is for;
b) why we should heed it.

- *Thinking back to previous studies, from what are we 'saved'?*

- *What will happen to those who don't respond in the way v13 recommends?*

GRASP

The 'Lord' is Jesus (see v9). His 'name' reveals his character as the one who rescues. As the rest of the Bible shows, 'calling on his name' means recognising who he is, personally turning to him, and saying words like: 'I'm sorry for opposing you. Thank you for dying in my place. I accept your gift of eternal life and recognise you're in charge.'

The result is that we are rescued (v13b) from God's anger and separation from him, and can be sure of a rescue by him on God's final judgement day. We're made one of his people.

But note two wrong moves to make:

First false move: trusting without turning ('I want my sins forgiven, but I want to keep living my way').
Second false move: turning without trusting ('I'm trying to live a better life, hoping God will accept me').

Becoming a Christian means turning from living for myself to living for Jesus as my Lord. Have you done that?

If yes, great! You have a secure relationship with God. Forever. And although you still sin, God won't reject or condemn you.

If no, why not?

SUMMARY

God rescues all who trust in the Lord Jesus.

APPLY

- *How have you responded to Jesus?*

- *What will it mean for you to live today with Jesus as Lord?*

GREAT NEWS
Section 1 re-cap

Let's pull all our summary lines from Section 1 together:

- God made the world and rules it.
- Every human being chooses to oppose God.
- God rightly separates us from him, now and forever.
- But that's not the end of the story.
- He sent Jesus to die, to be separated from God his Father, for us.
- God raised Jesus to declare him Rescuer and Lord of all.
- God rescues all who trust in the Lord Jesus.

Great news! What particularly strikes you this time?

IF…

If you've taken the step of turning back to God, trusting in Jesus' death in your place, and submitting to him as your Lord, then you are a Christian.

As a member of God's people, you're embarking on a lifetime with Jesus that will carry on into eternity.

IF…

If it feels like you're walking on air, then…great! But don't expect to do so all the time. And if it feels like not much has changed since you turned to Jesus, don't worry. Feelings change with the weather. They're unreliable.

Instead, trust the facts of Jesus' death in our place and his resurrection. And keep on living with Jesus as Lord. Things will begin to fall into place. The rest of **Start** will show you how to live as a Christian.

IF…

If you're thinking things over, then keep going. It's vital because your eternal future is at stake. Heaven and hell are realities. How will you respond to the Lord Jesus who died and was raised to life?

IF…

If you now have lots of questions, find Section 5 and then return to Section 2. Or quiz an older, wiser Christian friend. It will do him or her a power of good, too.

Face the music

Jesus made it crystal clear in his teaching what living with him as Lord would involve. He wanted to sort out those who were serious about following him and those who weren't.

All our readings in this section come from the Gospel of Luke.

Luke was a doctor who put together a carefully researched account of Jesus. His Gospel records what Jesus did, what he taught and what happened to him.

.... SECTION 2

FOLLOW... JESUS
Luke 9 v18-27

READ
Luke 9 v18-22.

Jesus is the Christ, the ruler sent by God to rescue people, as predicted in the Old Testament. But the disciples weren't to talk about Jesus until they knew what he'd come to do.

- *What did Jesus say had to happen to him (v22)?*

- *Knowing who Jesus is, how do you react to that?*

READ
Luke 9 v23-27.

ANSWER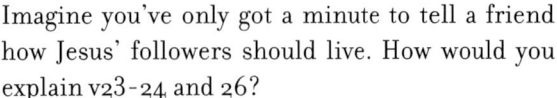
Imagine you've only got a minute to tell a friend how Jesus' followers should live. How would you explain v23-24 and 26?

- *What's the answer to the question in v25?*

- *When must we 'lose our lives' if we are to save them?*

- *When will our lives be saved?*

GRASP
To 'deny oneself' means to live for Jesus ('for me', v24) and not for yourself.

To 'take up the cross' means to walk in Jesus' footsteps: if you saw someone carrying a cross in those days, you wouldn't see him again. He was on his way to die.

Jesus wants disciples who daily give up their lives for him—doing what he wants—because he gave up his life for us.

- *How do you react to this?*

ANSWER
- *What else are we told about Jesus (v26b)?*

- *What's the warning for us in v26a?*

SUMMARY
Being a Christian means... following Jesus.

APPLY
- *What have you learnt today about living for Jesus?*

- *What changes will you need to make straight away?*

FOLLOW... NOW
Luke 9 v57-62

Luke has shown who Jesus is and why he came (Luke 9 v20-22). Here Jesus says more about the only way to follow him.

READ . . . .
Luke 9 v57-62.

ANSWER . . . .
Jot down what it would mean for each of the three characters here to follow Jesus:

  1
  2
  3

- As they meet Jesus, what do they have in common?

- What do Jesus' answers (v58, 60 and 62) have in common?

THINK . . . .
Consider what obeying these words might mean when there's a choice between being comfortable and following Jesus.

The first man preferred a secure way of life; the second wanted to complete his family duties; the third loved people at home.

Jesus isn't saying that homes and families aren't important.

- But what does he say (in v62) is the most important thing?

READ . . . .
v62 again.

- What's your response to this?

GRASP . . . .
When we realise how much Jesus has done for us, there's no other way but to follow him now and wholeheartedly, whatever that might mean we have to give up or miss out on.

- What could this involve for those who choose to follow Jesus?

SUMMARY . . . .
Being a Christian means...following Jesus now.

APPLY . . . .
- What are you ready to give up to follow Jesus? Income? Popularity? Good prospects? Possessions? Bad habits?

- What are you not yet prepared to give up?

- How have Jesus' words challenged you?

FOLLOW... THROUGH
Luke 12 v35-40

READ
Luke 12 v35-40.

ANSWER
Verses 35-38 describe servants waiting for their master to return from a wedding banquet. Verse 39 is the picture of a break-in.

Pick out the phrases which summarise Jesus' teaching here.

Complete this table using v40:

	Master	Servants
Identity:		
Task:		

GRASP
'Son of Man' was one of Jesus' favourite titles for himself. Taken from the Old Testament book of Daniel, it describes God's chosen king who comes to him to receive all authority for all time. Jesus is this 'Son of Man', who came to God the Father through his death, resurrection and return to heaven.

THINK
The Bible says that one day the Lord Jesus will come back to this earth to gather his people to himself and carry out his final judgement.

- Why must we be ready (v40)?

- What will be the result for those who are ready (v37-38)? When will this be?

Explain what's amazing about v37b.

Describe how you react to the prospect of Jesus' return:

○ Worried   ○ Excited   ○ Unprepared
Something else...

- How has today's teaching challenged you?

SUMMARY
Being a Christian means...following Jesus until he returns.

APPLY
Sometimes we prefer not think about Jesus' return because we're ashamed of the way we're living. Or we simply forget about it. Or we lose sight of what an exciting prospect it is (as v37).

Jesus will return in person. Every day brings that event closer.

- How should this change the way we...
  a) talk to Jesus now?

  b) live for him today?

- Will you ask Jesus to help you be ready?

FOLLOW... FIRST
Luke 14 v25-34

READ
Luke 14 v25-27.

ANSWER
- *What does v26 say it will take to be a disciple of Jesus?*

- *What attitude is required towards your family and yourself?*

Are we to hate our relatives? Sometimes that's all too easy. No. Jesus is saying: 'Your love for me must be so much greater that your love for your family will seem like hatred.'

Verse 27: In ancient times, a condemned criminal usually carried his own cross—to his death.

- *What is Jesus asking his disciples to do?*

READ
Luke 14 v28-35.

ANSWER
Try to re-tell the two stories in your own words (v28-30 and v31-32) to get them clear.
Then summarise their main point:

- *What will being a follower of Jesus mean for us and our possessions (v33)?*

GRASP
Is Jesus saying: 'Chuck it all away, then'? No...but it's more than simply being ready to give things up. It's doing it.

That's when it's real. Salt is only good if it's salty: a disciple is only a real one if he/she will give up anything to follow Jesus.

THINK
Jesus gave up his life to secure for us life forever with God.

- *What makes his request to follow him not unreasonable?*

- *What impact does this have on you?*

SUMMARY
Being a Christian means...following Jesus first.

APPLY
Will you make Jesus more important than your closest relationships (v26), what you own (v33), even your life (v27)?

- *What in practice will following Jesus mean for you?*

FACE THE MUSIC
Section 2 re-cap

Take the time to absorb what we've covered in Section 2. Read these verses and talk to God about your response.

FOLLOW JESUS
Luke 9 v23-25:
Then Jesus said to them all: 'If anyone would come after me, he must deny himself and take up his cross daily and follow me. For whoever wants to save his life will lose it, but whoever loses his life for me will save it. What good is it for a man to gain the whole world, and yet lose or forfeit his very self?'

FOLLOW NOW
Luke 9 v62:
Jesus replied: 'No-one who puts his hand to the plough and looks back is fit for service in the kingdom of God.'

FOLLOW THROUGH
Luke 12 v37 and 40:
'It will be good for those servants whose master finds them watching when he comes. I tell you the truth, he will dress himself to serve, will have them recline at the table and will come and wait on them.'

'You also must be ready, because the Son of Man will come at an hour when you do not expect him.'

FOLLOW FIRST
Luke 14 v33-34:
'In the same way, any of you who does not give up everything he has cannot be my disciple. Salt is good, but if it loses its saltiness, how can it be made salty again?'

Get up and grow

We trust you've done Sections 1 and 2. You've read about what God has done in Jesus and you've taken in Jesus' teaching. What you want to know now is... how to go on as a Christian, as one of God's people.

All our readings in this section are taken from the New Testament letter to the Colossians. The apostle Paul wanted to help Christians make progress—in what they knew and in the way they lived for Jesus.

.... SECTION 3

GO ON... WITH JESUS
Colossians 2 v6-8

READ
Colossians 2 v6-8 twice.

Verses 6-7 look back to all that Paul has said in chapters 1 and 2, and look ahead to what he will say in chapters 3 and 4. They act as a summary for the whole letter.

ANSWER
Pick out the main command in v6-7 (about five words long).
Now paraphrase it in less than ten words.

Think how you 'received Christ Jesus'.
- *What will 'continuing to live in him' involve?*

- *Can you summarise how to make progress as a Christian?*

THINK
See the 'just as...' (v6a)? Someone who's a Christian received Jesus by hearing the gospel and asking him to be their Lord. They handed over control of their life to him. We're to continue in that relationship with him, where we do what he wants.

ANSWER
Think how you would help someone understand the other phrases:
  'rooted and built up in him':
  'strengthened in the faith as you were taught':
  'overflowing with thankfulness':

THINK
Verse 8 issues an urgent warning to Christians.

- *What's the danger and how serious is it?*

- *Why must Christians not be distracted from Jesus?*

GRASP
'The faith' here means the gospel teaching about Jesus that the Colossians had heard. They were to grow in their understanding of it, and rely on it. It's the same for us: we need to get to know the gospel that Paul taught, that is written for us in the Bible.

SUMMARY
Being a Christian means... continuing with Jesus as Lord.

APPLY
- *Have you received Jesus properly—as Lord?*

- *Are you continuing to live 'in him'?*

GO ON... TO HEAVEN
Colossians 3 v1-11

READ
Colossians 3 v1-4.

ANSWER
Spot the command, expressed twice (v1, 2). What does it mean?

- *Why should Christians do this (v1a, 3b, 4)?*

If you're a Christian, there has been a decisive change in your life: you now share in Jesus' death and resurrection. Our old sinful personalities 'died' with Jesus and our lives are now with him in heaven.

- *How secure, then, are those who trust in Jesus?*

Use v1-4 to fill out the table:

What's true of Christians
Past
Present
Future

THINK
Trouble is, we've still got to live on earth before getting to heaven. So we need to put on the characteristics of heaven.

READ
Colossians 3 v5-11.

See what we're told to do, and why:

Pick out the commands:
    v5a
    v8
    9a

And the reasons given:
    v6
    v7
    v9b-10

GRASP
You're new people, Paul tells these Christians, being re-made to be like Jesus, who through his Spirit lives in you (v10-11). He helps us to stop doing what he doesn't like.

- *Which sin (or sins) listed in v5 do you need to kill off?*

- *What should motivate us to do this?*

- *How much is self-control a problem for you—as in v8?*

SUMMARY
Being a Christian means... shaping our lives for heaven.

APPLY
- *How can we appreciate more the truths of v1-4?*

- *What's your mind fixed on? What should it be?*

- *What's your worst habit? Will you cut it out?*

GO ON...
AMONG GOD'S PEOPLE
Colossians 3 v12-17

READ
Colossians 3 v12-14.

ANSWER
What's great about how Christians are described (v12a)?
- So how should we treat our fellow Christians (v12b-14)?

- What should constantly motivate us (v13b)?

GRASP
This is amazing: God says all who trust him have been chosen by him, are pure in his sight and close to his heart.

THINK
As a Christian, you've been born into a new family. There's no option but to get involved with it! The church is central in God's plans and crucial if you're to grow in faith—and help your Christian brothers and sisters grow too.

Think of three people you need to show compassion, kindness or patience to:

1   2   3

- How will you ensure you always act out of love?

READ
Colossians 3 v15-17.

ANSWER
- What should mark out the way we relate to each other (v15)?

- Why (v15b)?

- What should our conversations and meetings be like (v16)?

- How can we make sure the word of Christ dwells in us richly?

- What should characterize all our behaviour (v17)?

See the attitude that's mentioned in each of v15, 16 and 17?
- When might other people notice this in us? In you?

SUMMARY
Being a Christian means... being committed to God's people.

APPLY
- Do you belong to a church that teaches, believes and obeys the Bible? How can you build up those who are a part of it?

GO ON... IN LIFE
Colossians 3 v18 - 4 v1

READ
Colossians 3 v18-21.

ANSWER
Jot down your reaction to these verses.

- *According to these verses, how should a couple relate?*

- *How should parents and kids interact (v20-21)?*

- *What are the reasons given for this (v18b, 20b)?*

THINK
Are you single? Married? Got kids? Whatever your situation, think what a privilege it would be to be part of a family that operates like this to please the Lord Jesus (v18-21).

- *How will you work towards this ideal?*

- *What changes might you need to make straight away?*

GRASP
v20: children are to obey parents (assuming they're not commanding something the Bible prohibits). For how long? Until you're an adult, when you must honour them.

READ
Colossians 3 v22 - ch 4 v1.

Work includes paid/unpaid, voluntary/compulsory: all sorts of tasks we've got to do.

Find the verse in 3 v22 - 4 v1 which best summarises it all.

- *Who's watching as we work (v22-23)?*

- *How should this motivate us (v24-25)?*

There's a lesson for employers, too (4 v1), or those who have responsibility for others. What should they do, and why?

SUMMARY
Being a Christian means... pleasing Jesus at home and work.

APPLY
Home is a tough place to be a Christian. And work is often the last thing we want to do differently. Would you agree?

- *But what will stick with you from today's passage?*

GO ON...
WITH OUTSIDERS
Colossians 4 v2-6

READ
Colossians 4 v2-6.

REMEMBER
Paul wants Christians to talk to God about people (v2-4). And to talk to people about Jesus (v5-6).

- Even in prison, what's his over-riding concern (v3-4)?

'Mystery' (v3) doesn't mean (as we would say) a complete puzzle. No, it's something once hidden that is now out in the open. This is what Jesus has done: he has made God known, and knowable.

ANSWER
- What are the commands here (v2, 5, 6)?

- Which one do you think is hardest? Why?

THINK
How can we devote ourselves to prayer? (Hint: it's harder on your own.) Watch for things and people to pray for; and thank God as he answers those prayers.

ANSWER
- Who are the 'outsiders' (v4)?

- How should you behave towards them (v4)? Why?

- What should a Christian's conversation be like (v6)?

GRASP
Catch v6 again: be gracious in the way you talk to others, but salty too; be interesting, sparky and lead people to the gospel of Jesus.

Have a practice! Try to anticipate a chat you might have today with a non-Christian. What might you say about Jesus?

SUMMARY
Being a Christian means... talking to and about Jesus.

APPLY
Work out how you intend to make progress in prayer.

Think what changes you will make in: a) the way you behave among non-Christians; b) the way you talk to them.

Then ask for God's help in both areas.

GET UP AND GROW
Section 3 re-cap

Colossians says the way to make progress as a Christian is to learn what pleases the Lord Jesus and then to do it.

Ask God to help you with one particular area from this page:

GO ON WITH JESUS
Colossians 2 v6-7:
So then, just as you received Christ Jesus as Lord, continue to live in him, rooted and built up in him, strengthened in the faith as you were taught, and overflowing with thankfulness.

GO ON TO HEAVEN
Colossians 3 v1:
Since, then, you have been raised with Christ, set your hearts on things above, where Christ is seated at the right hand of God.

GO ON AMONG GOD'S PEOPLE
Colossians 3 v12:
Therefore, as God's chosen people, holy and dearly loved, clothe yourselves with compassion, kindness, humility, gentleness and patience.

GO ON IN LIFE
Colossians 3 v23-24:
Whatever you do, work at it with all your heart, as working for the Lord, not for men, since you know that you will receive an inheritance from the Lord as a reward. It is the Lord Christ you are serving.

GO ON WITH OUTSIDERS
Colossians 4 v2 and 5:
Devote yourselves to prayer, being watchful and thankful.

Be wise in the way you act towards outsiders; make the most of every opportunity.

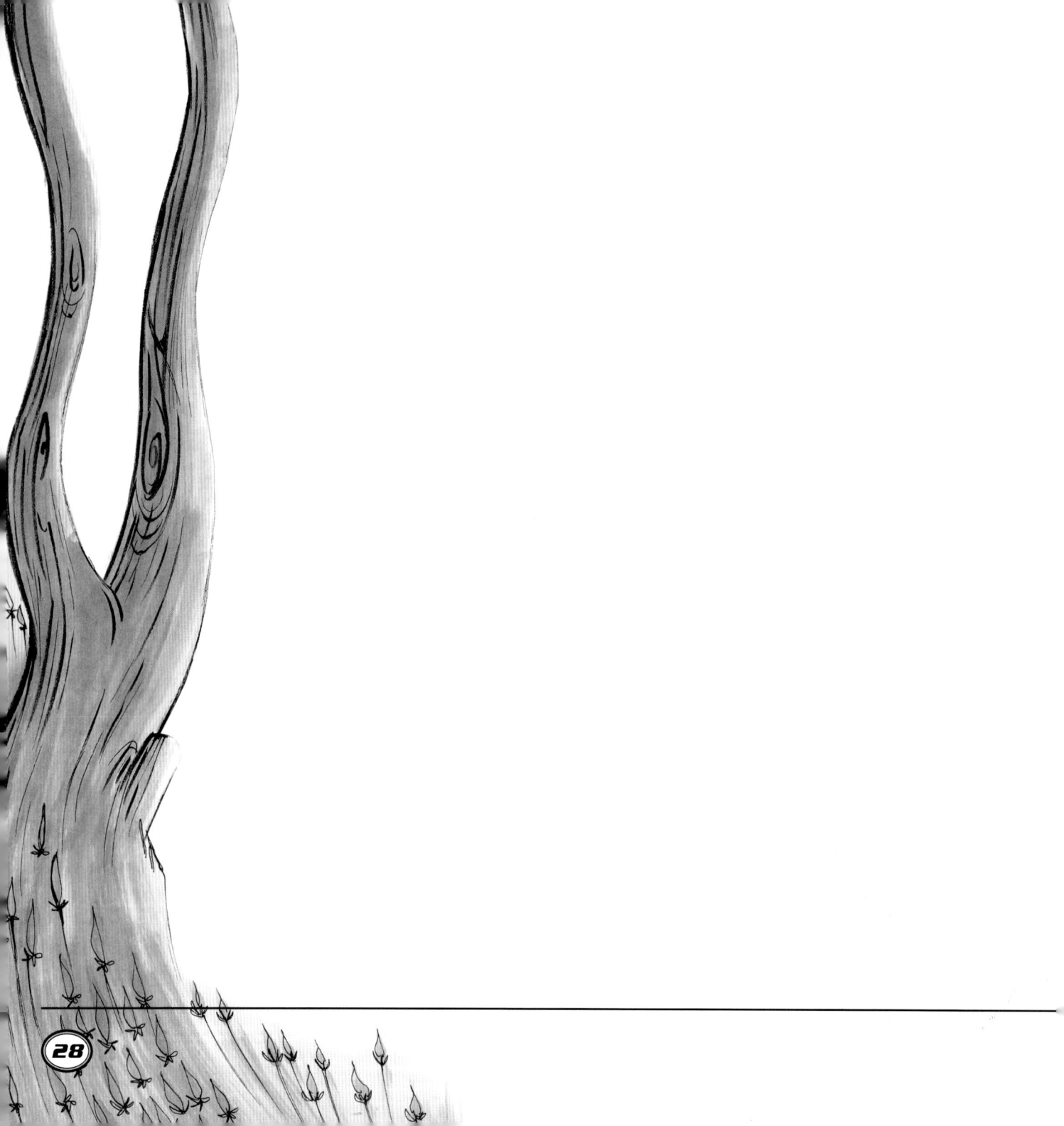

Great expectations

The last section showed how to make progress as a Christian, but what will the Christian life be like? What will living with Jesus as your Lord bring?

All our readings in this section are taken from the letter of 1 Peter. The apostle Peter wants Christians to have right expectations, so that they will trust Jesus and go on doing so.

.... SECTION 4

EXPECT... GRIEF
1 Peter 1 v1-9

READ

1 Peter 1 v1-2.

GRASP

As far as we can tell, Peter is writing mostly for 'exiled' Jews who are living far from their homeland of Israel. Through God's mercy, they have become Christians. He says that they have been: chosen by God in eternity, forgiven because of Jesus' death, made fit for God's presence by his Spirit, and called to obey Jesus.

These things are true for all who trust in Christ!

- *What's your reaction?*

Just like Peter's first readers, all Christians know that their real home is elsewhere, as Peter goes on to explain...

READ

1 Peter 1 v3-9.

ANSWER

Exciting! Jot down all the reasons given here as to why it's worth being a Christian:

- *What's your reaction to this?*

Christians look forward to their true home with God, where we belong. And we can be sure of making it (v5).

- *What more do we learn about living as a Christian (v6-7)?*

- *What should make Christians stand out (v8)? Why (v9)?*

THINK

'Grief in all kinds of trials' drives us to keep trusting Jesus. It proves our trust in God is genuine.

We don't see Jesus, but we believe in him, love him and are thrilled about the rescue he's achieved for us (v9).

SUMMARY

Christians expect... to suffer sadness to help us trust Jesus.

APPLY

- Do you see what Jesus' resurrection has ensured (v3-5)?

- Are you ready to suffer grief?

- Will you make sure it keeps you trusting Jesus?

EXPECT... CONFLICT
1 Peter 1 v13-16 and 2 v11-12

READ
1 Peter 1 v13-16.

ANSWER
- *What things does Peter tell his readers to do (v13)...*

  ... and not to do (v14)?

- *What's the motivation for behaving like this (v15)?*

READ
1 Peter 2 v11-12.

ANSWER
v11: 'aliens' = living far from home; v12: 'pagans' = non-Christians.

- *What does Peter tell his readers to avoid (v11)...*

  ... and to get on with (v12a)?

- *What's the motivation for behaving like this (v12b)?*

Now pick up the connection between 1 v14 and 2 v11:

- *So what will the Christian life be like?*

GRASP
Christians face an ongoing fight against sin in our lives. Since Jesus is our Lord, we seek to obey him, not our own selfish desires, which still persist after we've turned to Jesus.

Christians also face the likelihood of opposition from non-believers. See what form it might take (2 v12).

Now pick up the connection between 1 v13b and 2 v12b:

- *What should dominate our thinking?*

We know Jesus has promised to come back, so we live our lives keenly aware of that fact.

SUMMARY
Christians expect... to fight sin and to face opposition.

APPLY
- *What sinful desires do you need to do battle with?*

- *What will you remember if you start to be opposed?*

EXPECT... SUFFERING
1 Peter 4 v12-19

READ
1 Peter 4 v12-19.

THINK
Why does Peter keep talking so much about suffering?

ANSWER
Divide up the verses into two groups, those that give:

a) warning **b) encouragement**

- How should v12-13 change our attitude to suffering?

Make sure you have taken this in—because if things are easy now, then you'll need to remind yourself of this in future.

Seems crazy: that Christians should praise God for their suffering. Now get the other reasons why:
v14
v16
v17-18

GRASP
v17-18: if life's tough for us, think how much worse it will be for those who don't obey God's command to trust in Jesus.

- Does this change your attitude? How?

- What's a right way to go forward then as a Christian (v19)?

GRASP
Peter doesn't want his readers to say: 'We never realised that being a Christian would be as tough as this'. Christians will share in Jesus' sufferings: a case of suffering before glory.

So, imagine when someone laughs at you, or spreads lies about you, or even chucks a brick through your window, just because you're a Christian.

- How will you be tempted to react?

- How will you, with God's help, seek to react from now on?

SUMMARY
Christians expect... to suffer specifically for being Christians.

APPLY
- What's your attitude to suffering?

- What do today's verses say it should be?

EXPECT... TEMPTATION
1 Peter 5 v8-11

READ
1 Peter 5 v8-9.

ANSWER
You're asked by a friend: 'What can I expect as a Christian?' Using v8-9, begin all your answers with: 'Be ready for…'

- What might you notice if someone's a Christian (v8a)?

- Why do Christians need to be like this (v8b)?

THINK
Peter is convinced the devil is real all right. And that he's out to devour people—to tear them away from trusting Christ and living with him as Lord.

Now explain the only way to respond (v9a).

- What will this mean in practice?

- What should motivate us to do this (v9b)?

GRASP
We're to resist the devil. When temptations come our way to do things that displease Jesus and hurt others, then look to God and say 'no' to that temptation. It's nothing more dramatic than that. Simply resist the devil and move on.

READ
1 Peter 5 v10-11.

ANSWER
Notice as many encouragements as you can find in v10.

GRASP
Peter says they'll only suffer 'a little while'. In fact, he's talking about the whole of their earthly lives. But our lifetimes are nothing compared with sharing in the presence and greatness of Jesus forever.

SUMMARY
Christians expect… to battle against constant temptation.

APPLY

- Will you work at being self-controlled and alert?

- Will you take today's warnings seriously?

- How will v10 help you when living for Christ is hard?

GREAT EXPECTATIONS
Section 4 re-cap

What is the Christian life going to be like?
Look out for the privileges and warnings in these reminders:

EXPECT GRIEF
1 Peter 1 v3-6:
Praise be to the God and Father of our Lord Jesus Christ! In his great mercy he has given us new birth into a living hope through the resurrection of Jesus Christ from the dead, and into an inheritance that can never perish, spoil or fade—kept in heaven for you, who through faith are shielded by God's power until the coming of the salvation that is ready to be revealed in the last time.

In this you greatly rejoice, though now for a little while, you may have had to suffer grief in all kinds of trials.

EXPECT CONFLICT
1 Peter 2 v11-12:
Dear friends, I urge you as aliens and strangers in the world, to abstain from sinful desires, which war against your soul. Live such good lives among the pagans that, though they accuse you of doing wrong, they may see your good deeds and glorify God on the day he visits us.

EXPECT SUFFERING
1 Peter 4 v12-13:
Dear friends, do not be surprised at the painful trial you are suffering, as though something strange were happening to you. But rejoice that you participate in the sufferings of Christ, so that you may be overjoyed when his glory is revealed.

EXPECT TEMPTATION
1 Peter 5 v8-9:
Be self-controlled and alert. Your enemy the devil prowls around like a roaring lion looking for someone to devour. Resist him, standing firm in the faith, because you know that your brothers throughout the world are undergoing the same kind of sufferings.

Help!

In this section, we've included answers to questions that are commonly asked about God, Jesus, the Bible, the dilemmas of suffering and human nature, becoming a Christian and living as a Christian.

We're aware that our answers are brief and that there will also be questions that you would like answers to that we haven't included. Make sure you quiz an older, wiser Christian about them—or drop us a line. You'll find our address at the back.

If you're using this book in a pair or as a group, why not discuss first how you would answer the questions?

.... SECTION 5

ON... GOD
Help i

1. DOES GOD EXIST?
Let's consider the evidence:

a) the world
Think of the size of the earth, planets, galaxies... the beauty and detail of nature... the incredible design of a human being... doesn't it begin to point us to a Creator?

b) ourselves
Why are humans restless? Why do we long to sort out life's big questions? What about your conscience and in-built sense of right and wrong? Where does all this come from?

c) the Bible
Genesis 1 v1 starts: 'In the beginning, God...' The Bible takes it as a fact that God exists and lays the evidence before us. Will you check out the Bible's reliability?

d) our experience
Christians down the centuries have said that God speaks to them as they read the Bible. Isn't this worth at least investigating?

e) Jesus in history
Jesus claimed to reveal God to the world—in his teaching, his actions, his character and chiefly in his death and resurrection. The Bible says Jesus came into the world to make God known, and to make it possible for us to know him. If God's gone to great lengths to reveal himself, it would be foolish to ignore that. Wouldn't it?

Check also answers on Jesus and the Bible (Help ii and iii).

2. HOW DO WE KNOW WHAT GOD IS LIKE?
Recall point 1(e) above. If God has revealed himself through Jesus (and therefore through the Bible), then we're not left to make guesses about God; i.e., if you want to know what God is like, look at Jesus. We can't decide what we want God to be like: we have to accept him as he's revealed himself.

Remember Section 1 ('Great News')? That shows us the ruling Creator God, totally pure, who must judge wrongdoing, yet completely loving and faithful. He's the God who sent his Son Jesus to die so that we could come into the presence of God forever. *That's* the God revealed to us.

On both questions 1 and 2, Psalm 19 says that God's world (v1-6) and God's word (v7-14) show us what God is like. Read it!

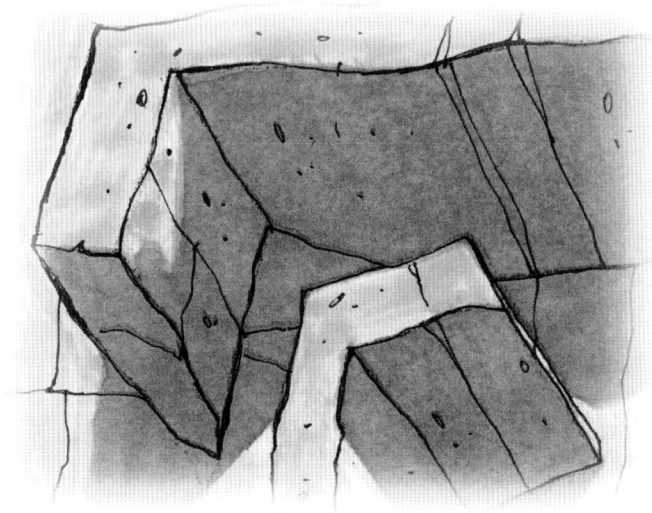

ON... JESUS
Help ii

1. DID JESUS REALLY EXIST?

There's little room for saying Jesus never existed. Consider:

a) The New Testament
Matthew, Mark, Luke and John (and all the New Testament writers) tell us he did;

b) Non-Christian authors
Roman authors Tacitus (55-120AD), Suetonius (69-140AD) and Pliny (61-113AD) mention Jesus and the first Christians, as does the Jewish historian Josephus (37-100AD).

2. CAN WE TRUST WHAT THE NEW TESTAMENT SAYS ABOUT HIM?

The question could be put another way: 'Have Matthew and Mark and the others just made it all up about Jesus?' If so, it's just like fairy stories and can be dismissed. Can it? Consider:

i) The Gospel writers' methods
See, for example, Luke 1 v1-4. They wrote their Gospels after much research, based on eye-witness reports.

ii) Their style
They included quirky details or difficult material. If they wanted to make things up, it would have been easy to omit this.

iii) Their lives
They were prepared to suffer and die to stand by their message and their Master, Jesus. Would they really have done this if it was all a lie?

iv) Their motives
They wanted others to be convinced about Jesus (see, for example, John 20 v31), so they took care to present what was true.

v) The timing
All four Gospels were written close in time to the events they describe. So the writers would have been accountable to eye-witnesses. In fact, the whole New Testament was complete by AD100 (at the very latest), and that sort of timing is remarkable for documents in the ancient world.

vi) Archaeology
This consistently backs up events recorded in the Bible.

Put the evidence together and it's overwhelming: we can trust what the New Testament says about Jesus. Since Jesus did exist in history, he becomes very hard to ignore. This Jesus, who revealed God to the world and died and rose again, is alive now and calling for us to turn to him and live for him.

ON... THE BIBLE
Help iii

1. CAN WE TRUST THE BIBLE?
Let's consider:

a) Jesus' view
Jesus referred to the Old Testament as God's word (e.g., John 10 v35) and said that his own words (recorded in the Gospels for us) would last forever (e.g., Mark 13 v31).

b) the apostles' view
The apostles—those who went round with Jesus and were sent by him to be his messengers—recognised the Bible as trustworthy (e.g., 2 Timothy 3 v16) and knew their own words to be God's words too (e.g., 1 Thessalonians 2 v13).

c) One message
The Bible has 66 books written over 1,500 years, with 40 authors in 3 languages, but it has one central message, pointing consistently to Jesus.

d) Bible prophecy
In the Old Testament, spokesmen for God made predictions, chiefly about Jesus. He fulfilled more than 300 prophecies, including 29 on the day he died.

e) Its authority
Christians say they know the Bible to be trustworthy: it makes sense of God, the world and ourselves, and rings true in our experience, speaking with authority.

So let's trust the Bible and get into it.

2. WHAT ON EARTH DO I DO WITH THE BIBLE?
Baffled as to where to start? Remember:

a) It's all about Jesus
The Old Testament prepares us for the coming of Jesus; the New Testament records and explains it (e.g., Luke 24 v27 and 44). So whichever bit of the Bible you're reading, ask: 'What more does this teach me about Jesus?'

b) It's written for you
The Bible is for everyone, whatever you're like, and speaks clearly. No need to think that it's somehow too complicated.

c) Get into it
Colossians 3 v16 (remember Section 2?) urges us to let God's word 'dwell in us richly' as Christians meet together. Will you find ways of getting regular input from the Bible?

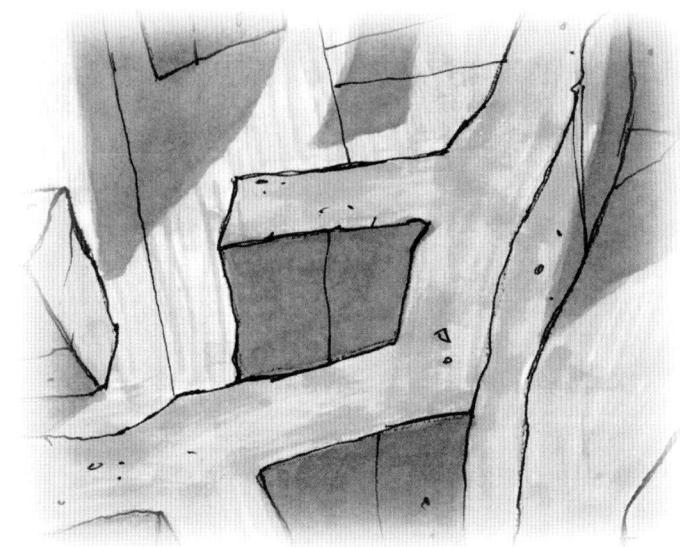

ON... DILEMMAS
Help iv

1. HOW CAN THERE BE A GOD OF LOVE WHEN THERE'S SO MUCH SUFFERING IN THE WORLD?

A question like this can make us think:
- a) Surely God can't exist then;
- b) If God exists and he's loving, then he must be powerless;
- c) If God exists, and there's so much suffering, then he can't be loving at all.

What clues does the Bible give to answer this?

a) We're not excused
Humans are to blame for a large slice of the world's suffering. Each of us has caused other people pain and failed to help.

b) The world's not right
Natural disasters can be traced back to the time when human beings first opposed God's rule. That rebellion affected not just us, but the whole world. Earthquakes and the like painfully remind us that sin has spoilt everything.

c) God is not remote from suffering
His own Son, Jesus, endured the most unimaginable suffering: death on a cross, under the punishment of God his Father, separated from him—for us.

d) God uses suffering
Hard times make us think about what really counts in life and help Christians grow more like Jesus; pain can be good for us.

e) God will end suffering
God has promised that in his new heaven and earth there will be no more pain, grief or tears. What a prospect!

Check also answers under God (Help i) and 'Expect... suffering' (in Section 4).

2. AREN'T I GOOD ENOUGH FOR GOD ALREADY?

(i.e., 'Why do I need Jesus? Of course, God will accept me.')

The Bible says that such a view:

a) overestimates our own goodness
We are not basically good at heart, but corrupt in our attitudes, actions and motives. Even our best actions derive from mixed motives. We each choose to live in opposition to God, living life our own way.

b) underestimates God's holiness
He cannot tolerate wrongdoing; he must act to judge all evil. His standards are far higher than we dare to think.

c) ignores the gospel
God sent his Son Jesus to die on a cross to rescue us. If we were good enough for God already, why would God go to such lengths?

The right response is to remember we're not rescued for heaven by doing good deeds, but solely by relying on what Jesus has done.

Check also answers under Becoming a Christian (Help v), and all of Great News (Section 1).

ON... BECOMING A CHRISTIAN
Help v

1. WHAT'S BECOMING A CHRISTIAN ALL ABOUT?

Section 1 will help (as will Romans 10 v12-13). Becoming a Christian is about turning and trusting: turning to submit to the Lord Jesus and trusting in his death. It involves:

a) Saying sorry

We're to apologise personally and wholeheartedly for opposing God and trying to live as if he didn't exist or rule.

b) Saying thank you

We should thank God for sending Jesus into the world to die, separated from God his Father. On the cross, he died in our place, taking the punishment of God for us.

c) Saying please

We need to turn from living life our own way to ask Jesus to be our own Lord and Rescuer. We trust that his death is all that's needed to put us right with God.

2. HOW DO I KNOW IF I TOOK THAT STEP PROPERLY?

It's worth doing the following:

a) Check

What makes you ask this question? Is it because things don't feel much different or haven't changed much since you decided to become a Christian? Well, feelings aren't incidental, but trust facts first. If you've turned to Jesus and are trusting in the cross, then a lot has changed, even though some days it might not feel like it. Now get going—Section 3 will help.

b) Think

It's easy to make two mistakes here:

  i) to think you are a Christian when you're not. Have you actually, personally turned to Jesus? If so, great!

  ii) to think you're not a Christian when you are. It's not very helpful to over-analyse what you've done. Simply ask: 'Who am I trusting now to get me to heaven—myself or Jesus?' If the answer is Jesus, take heart and continue with him as Lord.

c) Remember

The best evidence that you've taken that step properly is that you keep on trusting Jesus. Are you doing so? Then be encouraged and keep going.

Check also answers under Living as a Christian (Help vi).

ON... LIVING AS A CHRISTIAN
Help vi

1. CAN I BE SURE I'M A CHRISTIAN?

Yes! The Bible wants those who trust in Christ to enjoy the certainty of knowing that eternal life is theirs.

Look at God's work in your life, and over time you should be able to detect a changed attitude towards Jesus, towards sin and towards God's people.

So, ask yourself:

a) Am I personally trusting in Jesus, God's Son, and his death to bring me forgiveness?

b) Do I care what Jesus would think of the way I behave?

c) Does it bother me if a Christian friend decides they don't want to live as a Christian any more?

If the answers are 'Yes', then be thankful and keep going.

All our answers here are drawn from the letter of 1 John. You'll find 1 John 5 v11-13 helpful here.

It's worth pointing out that there's no offer of assurance for those who persist in disobeying God.

2. WHAT IF I SIN REALLY BADLY?

The Bible says Jesus' death on the cross cleanses us from every sin (past, present and future). Jesus promises to forgive all who turn to him. It will help to do two things:

a) Remember

The cross removes the penalty of sin (condemnation by God) and breaks the power of sin in our lives (so it doesn't rule us). But when we turn to Christ, the presence of sin remains. So there'll always be a fight on within us. If you're aware of this conflict and are seeking God's help in it, that's a good sign.

b) Repent

When we sin, as we sadly will do, it doesn't break our relationship with God, but spoils it. We don't have to become a Christian all over again, we simply need to turn back to him and confess our sin. The Bible promises he will forgive us. You'll find 1 John 1 v5-10 (especially v9) helpful here.

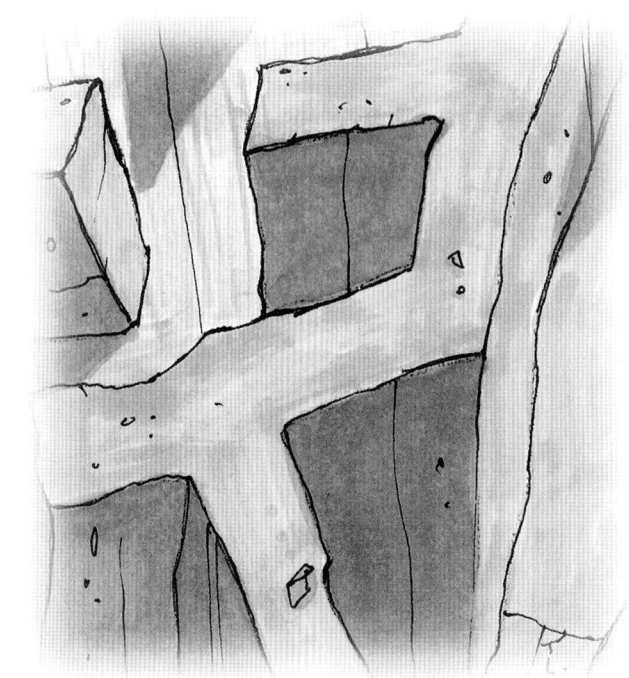

WHERE NOW?
The last word

Thank you for using **Start**. We trust you found it helpful.

If you're to grow as a Christian, living with Jesus as Lord, it will help to keep on getting regular input from the Bible. So…

1) commit yourself to a local church where the Bible is taught, applied and obeyed;

2) keep reading the Bible for yourself.

See the page opposite for some resources and further reading that will help.